孝經

The Classic of Filial Respect

孝 經

The Classic of Filial Respect

Published and translated by:

Buddhist Text Translation Society
1777 Murchison Drive
Burlingame, CA 94010-4504
www.drba.org

Buddhist Text Translation Society
Dharma Realm Buddhist University
Dharma Realm Buddhist Association

11 10 09   10 9 8 7 6 5 4 3 2 1

ISBN 978-986-7328-44-1
Printed in Taiwan

身體髮膚，受之父母，
不敢毀傷，孝之始也。

Every part of our bodies, even the hair and skin, is derived from our parents; therefore, we should protect our bodies and keep them from injury; this is the fundamental act of filial respect.

Content 目錄

重譯《孝經》序　Preface

2003暑假於佛根地道場(奧雷根州)，從書架上偶然拾起兩本好書：
　　一、《左傳》
　　(英譯版；哥倫比亞大學出版社，1989)
　　二、《孝經》
　　(雙語版；聖約翰大學出版社出版，1961)

In 2003 when I had a chance to go to the Buddha Root Farm (one of our Dharma Realm Buddhist Association branch temples in Oregon), I picked up from the bookshelf two good books:
1) *The Tso Chuan* (Columbia University Press, 1989)
2) *The Hsiao Jing* (St. John University Press, 1961)

此《孝經》雖則薄薄的一本，譯文卻清新雋永，故印象特別深刻；又回想起　宣公上人處處現身行孝，垂範後世，就帶回萬佛城。之後一、兩年間，總有一個願望：想跟聖約翰大學出版社聯繫，問為何都已三、四十年了，怎麼都沒聽說你們再版過？你們若不出版，可否允許版權轉讓，讓有心人來出版？幾次試著接洽，終以無功而返。

The *Hsiao Jing* (*Xiao Jing*) was a thin and old book, yet its translation was quite impressive - fresh and profound. Recalling the Venerable Master Hua's exemplary conduct of filial piety, I brought it back to the City of Ten Thousand Buddhas (CTTB). Later, I had a sincere wish to contact St. John University Press to suggest that this book be republished - it seems that 40 some years have passed without anyone else publishing this book. My several attempts were of no avail.

2006「法總」決定將「萬佛聖城」30週年慶延後三年到2009年；2006 - 2007 年「培德中學」跟進全美許多中學，首設 AP Chinese (高級中文)課程。班上有劉親智、謝阜庭等六個孩子，這時萌生一念：《孝經》既然不長，求人不如求己，讓六個孩子(我戲稱他們為「AP 六君子」)一人翻三篇，一學年一定搞定的。且萬佛城慶 30 週年之際，若是校友重逢，回首當年他們一起翻譯過的《孝經》，這不是給聖城最好的一個禮物嗎？

In 2006, an important decision was made within DRBA to postpone the celebration of the 30th anniversary of the City of Ten Thousand Buddhas to 2009. Also, in the 2006-07 school year, the Developing Virtue Secondary School followed the trend of high schools throughout the United States to set up an AP Chinese course in the curriculum. In my AP Chinese class there were six students: Michael Hsieh, Qin Zhi Lau, Alex Aw, Sunny Chye, Chris Zhao, and Jimbo Kuo.

While teaching, a new idea flashed through my mind: Rather than seeking from others, why not do it ourselves? Since the eighteen chapters are all quite short, if each one of my students does three chapters, then in one year, this book will be done. Also, when they come back in 2009, wouldn't it be meaningful to see the book that was the result of their collective efforts and team spirit? And wouldn't this the best present for CTTB's 30 anniversary that we - the teacher and the students - can offer to CTTB?

This is the origin of the re-translation of *Xiao Jing*.

孔子說這孝是一切德之本，是一切教之源，是天之經、地之義。宣公上人也說「一切教不離開孝」，孝這一門課，總括「無邊無際的課」。在 1983 年 7 月 29 日開示中又提到「孝」在「世間法中是木本水源，應該慎終追遠，孝順父母，恭敬師長，這是天經地義之事」。這與孔子所教遙相呼應。如今人心不古日甚，孝道不彰已久，祈藉此《孝經》之重譯，一則略略喚醒已在「天下熙熙，皆為利來；天下攘攘，皆為利往」中忙昏了頭的人們；二則以「孝道」這一門課與所有學子共勉，將修圓滿，是為至盼。

Confucius mentioned that filial piety is the foundation of all virtues, the source of teachings, the guidance of Heaven, and the principle of the earth. Venerable Master Hua also said that "all teachings are not apart from *Xiao* - filial respect." *Xiao,* as a study, contains "limitless studies." In his instructional talk given on the 29th of July, 1983 in the CTTB he also said that *Xiao*, within the mundane dharmas, is the root or the fountainhead. We should be filial to our parents as well as to our teachers and elders. This is the what is right and proper to do." This exactly echoes what Confucius taught in the distant past. Now it is a time of ever-declining for public morality, and the path of *Xiao* has not been taken seriously or advocated for a long time. Hence by translating and publishing this *Xiao Jing*, we first wish to awake up a little bit those who have been so busy in their profit-seeking that they almost forget about themselves; second, we wish to encourage that everyone, especially students, can study and practice *Xiao* to perfection.

Jin Yan Shr Oct. 25, 2008

釋 近嚴 謹識

公元 二〇〇八年十月二十五

佛曆 三〇三五年十月二十五

開宗明義章第一

Chapter 1: Overall Principles at the Beginning

仲尼居，曾子侍。子曰：「先王有至德要道，以順天下，民用和睦，上下無怨。汝知之乎？」曾子避席曰：「參不敏，何足以知之！」子曰：「夫孝，德之本也，教之所由生也。復坐！吾語汝。身體髮膚，受之父母，不敢毀傷，孝之始也。立身行道，揚名於後世，以顯父母，孝之終也。夫孝，始於事親，中於事君，終於立身。《大雅》云：『無念爾祖，聿修厥德。』」

Confucius was at leisure and his disciple Zeng Zi was attending upon him. Confucius said, "The ancient sage-rulers possessed the utmost virtues and essential Way, with which they ruled the nation, and as a result people lived harmoniously, and neither the nobility nor the commoners had any grievance. Do you know about it?"

Zeng Zi rose from his seat and said, "How could I, Shen*, who is dull-witted, know about it?"

Confucius continued, "Filial respect is the foundation of all virtue, and the source of all teachings. Be seated, and I will explain to you. Every part of our bodies, even the hair and skin, is derived from our parents; therefore, we should protect our bodies and keep them from injury; this is the fundamental act of filial respect. We establish ourselves by practicing the Way so that we can leave a good name for future generations. Thus, we honor and glorify our parents; this is the ultimate act of filial respect. To practice filial respect, we begin by serving our parents, followed by serving the sovereign, and finally by establishing ourselves well. As it is said in the *Major Odes (of The Book of Poetry)*:

> *How can you not be mindful of your ancestors*
> *And not cultivate your virtues to safeguard theirs?"*

Notes:

*Shen is the name by which Zeng Shen refers to himself.

❶ 開宗明義：孝經首章篇名。說明全書宗旨義理。開，張也；宗，本也；明，顯也；義，理也。

❷ 先王：古代聖王。或稱已故的君王。

❸ 曾子：（公元前505～公元前436年），名參，字子輿，春秋末魯國人。事親至孝。十六歲拜孔子為師，勤奮好學，頗得孔子真傳。

❹ 立身：建立自身做人處世的基礎。

❺ 聿：發語詞，用於句首或句中，無義。

❻ 厥：他的、那個。同 "其"。

天子章第二

Chapter 2: The Son of Heaven

子ㄗˇ曰ㄩㄝ：「愛ㄞˋ親ㄑㄧㄣ者ㄓㄜˇ，不ㄅㄨˋ敢ㄍㄢˇ惡ㄜˋ於ㄩˊ人ㄖㄣˊ；敬ㄐㄧㄥˋ親ㄑㄧㄣ者ㄓㄜˇ，不ㄅㄨˋ敢ㄍㄢˇ慢ㄇㄢˋ於ㄩˊ人ㄖㄣˊ。愛ㄞˋ敬ㄐㄧㄥˋ盡ㄐㄧㄣˋ於ㄩˊ事ㄕˋ親ㄑㄧㄣ，而ㄦˊ德ㄉㄜˊ教ㄐㄧㄠˋ加ㄐㄧㄚ於ㄩˊ百ㄅㄞˇ姓ㄒㄧㄥˋ，刑ㄒㄧㄥˊ於ㄩˊ四ㄙˋ海ㄏㄞˇ，蓋ㄍㄞˋ天ㄊㄧㄢ子ㄗˇ之ㄓ孝ㄒㄧㄠˋ也ㄧㄝˇ。《甫ㄈㄨˇ刑ㄒㄧㄥˊ》云ㄩㄣˊ：『一ㄧ人ㄖㄣˊ有ㄧㄡˇ慶ㄑㄧㄥˋ，兆ㄓㄠˋ民ㄇㄧㄣˊ賴ㄌㄞˋ之ㄓ。』」

The Master said, "One who loves his parents does not dare to be contemptuous of others. One who respects his parents does not dare to be arrogant towards others. When a king or prince perfectly fulfills his love and respect for his parents, his virtue and teachings will influence the people and set a high standard for everyone throughout the nation. This is the filial respect of the Son of Heaven. The *Code of Fu* says:

When the Son of Heaven is virtuous,
Millions of people will rely on his blessings from Heaven."

Notes:

❶ 甫刑：① 即《尚書·呂刑》。周穆王時有關刑罰的文告，由呂侯請命而頒，後因呂侯後代改封甫侯，故《呂刑》又稱《甫刑》。② 借指周代刑法。

❷ 一人有慶，兆民賴之：帝王的善績福祚，是百姓所仰賴的。

諸侯章第三

Chapter 3: The Feudal Lords

在上不驕，高而不危；制節謹度，滿而不溢。高而不危，所以長守貴也。滿而不溢，所以長守富也。富貴不離其身，然後能保其社稷，而和其民人，蓋諸侯之孝也。《詩》云：『戰戰兢兢，如臨深淵，如履薄冰。』

"To avoid the precariousness of high position, a feudal lord should not be arrogant. He should be cautious in observing the rules and laws, and prudent in spending, so that 'the water may be filled to the brim without overflowing.'

"To dwell on high without peril is the way to preserve one's nobility. To be 'full without overflowing' is the way to preserve one's wealth. When the feudal lord retains his nobility and wealth, he thereby preserves the altar of his land and granary, and secures the harmony of his people. This is the filial respect of a feudal lord. As it is said in the *Book of Poetry*:

Be apprehensive, be cautious
As if standing on the brink of a deep abyss,
As if treading upon thin ice."

Notes:

❶ 社_{shè}稷_{jì}：本_{běn}指_{zhǐ}土_{tǔ}神_{shén}和_{hé}穀_{gǔ}神_{shén}，後_{hòu}指_{zhǐ}國_{guó}家_{jiā}。

❷ 戰_{zhàn}戰_{zhàn}兢_{jīng}兢_{jīng}：因_{yīn}畏_{wèi}懼_{jù}而_{ér}顫_{zhàn}抖_{dǒu}。形_{xíng}容_{róng}戒_{jiè}懼_{jù}謹_{jǐn}慎_{shèn}的_{de}樣_{yàng}子_{zi}。

卿大夫章第四

Chapter 4: High Government Officials

非fēi 先xiān 王wáng 之zhī 法fǎ 服fú 不bù 敢gǎn 服fú ， 非fēi 先xiān 王wáng
之 法 言 不 敢 道 ， 非 先 王 之 德 行
不 敢 行 。 是 故 非 法 不 言 ， 非 道
不 行 ； 口 無 擇 言 ， 身 無 擇 行 。
言 滿 天 下 無 口 過 ， 行 滿 天 下 無
怨 惡 。 三 者 備 矣 ， 然 後 能 守 其
宗 廟 ， 蓋 卿 大 夫 之 孝 也 。 《 詩
》 云 ： 『 夙 夜 匪 懈 ， 以 事 一 人
。 』

"He dares not wear clothing that is censured by the ancient sage-kings; he dares not utter words that are censured by them; he dares not do any deed that is not in the manner of their virtuous conduct.

"Therefore, he does not utter words that are not in accordance with propriety; he avoids conduct that is not in accordance with the Way.

"Therefore, his words and conduct will effortlessly mesh with the rules and standards.

"Thus, with faultless speech, his words spread throughout the four directions; with blameless behavior, his conduct is widely known without rousing resentment or aversion. When these three aspects (of dress, speech, and conduct) are all perfect, then one can preserve one's ancestral temple. This is the filial repect of a high government official. As it is said in the *Book of Poetry:*

Never idle, day or night,
He is always diligent in his service of duty."

Notes:

❶ 口 無 擇 言 ， 身 無 擇 行 ： 口 無 敗 言 ， 身 無 敗 行 。
說 話 做 事 ， 皆 合 道 理 ， 無 需 經 過 選 擇 。

士章第五

Chapter 5: Civil Servants

資 zī 於 yú 事 shì 父 fù 以 yǐ 事 shì 母 mǔ ， 而 ér 愛 ài 同 tóng ； 資 zī 於 yú 事 shì 父 fù 以 yǐ 事 shì 君 jūn ， 而 ér 敬 jìng 同 tóng 。 故 gù 母 mǔ 取 qǔ 其 qí 愛 ài ， 而 ér 君 jūn 取 qǔ 其 qí 敬 jìng ， 兼 jiān 之 zhī 者 zhě 父 fù 也 yě 。 故 gù 以 yǐ 孝 xiào 事 shì 君 jūn ， 則 zé 忠 zhōng ； 以 yǐ 敬 jìng 事 shì 長 zhǎng ， 則 zé 順 shùn 。 忠 zhōng 順 shùn 不 bù 失 shī ， 以 yǐ 事 shì 其 qí 上 shàng ， 然 rán 後 hòu 能 néng 保 bǎo 其 qí 祿 lù 位 wèi ， 而 ér 守 shǒu 其 qí 祭 jì 祀 sì ， 蓋 gài 士 shì 之 zhī 孝 xiào 也 yě 。 《 詩 shī 》 云 yún ： 『 夙 sù 興 xīng 夜 yè 寐 mèi ， 無 wú 忝 tiǎn 爾 ěr 所 suǒ 生 shēng 。 』

"Affection is a common attribute in serving one's father and mother; and reverence is a common attribute in serving one's father and one's sovereign. Therefore, one serves one's mother with affection, and one's ruler with reverence. Both attributes are applied when one serves one's father.

"Therefore, to be filial to one's sovereign is to be loyal; to be respectful towards one's elders is to comply with their wishes.

Both loyalty and compliance must not be lacking when serving one's superiors so that one is able to preserve one's salary and position, and carry on the rites of sacrifices. Such is the filial respect of a civil servant. As it is said in the *Book of Poetry:*

> *Rising early and retiring late,*
> *I dare not disgrace those who gave me life."*

Notes:

❶ 夙興夜寐：早起晚睡。比喻勤勞。

❷ 忝：羞辱、汙衊。

庶人章第六

Chapter 6: The Common People

yòng tiān zhī dào fēn dì zhī lì jǐn shēn jié

用天之道，分地之利，謹身節

yòng yǐ yàng fù mǔ cǐ shù rén zhī xiào yě

用，以養父母，此庶人之孝也

gù zì tiān zǐ zhì yú shù rén xiào wú zhōng

。故自天子至於庶人，孝無終

shǐ ér huàn bù jí zhě wèi zhī yǒu yě

始，而患不及者，未之有也。

"By according with way of Heaven and discerning the advantages afforded by Earth, one is cautious and frugal so as to be able to provide for one's parents-such is the filial respect of the common people. From the Son of Heaven to the populace, filial respect should be practiced at every level of the society. It is a deed that everyone is capable of practicing. "

Notes:

❶ 庶人（shù rén）：古代平民之稱（gǔ dài píng mín zhī chēng）。

❷ 患（huàn）：擔心（dān xīn）。

❸ 不及（bù jí）：做不到（zuò bú dào）。

❹ 孝無終始（xiào wú zhōng shǐ）：亦作（yì zuò）「孝無貴賤」（xiào wú guì jiàn），行孝無貴賤之別（xíng xiào wú guì jiàn zhī bié）。

三才章第七

Chapter 7: The Three Forces

曾子曰：「甚哉，孝之大也！」子曰：「夫孝，天之經也，地之義也，民之行也。天地之經，而民是則之。則天之明，因地之利，以順天下，是以其教不肅而成，其政不嚴而治。先王見教之可以化民也，是故先之以博愛，而民莫遺其親，陳之以德義，而民興行；先之以敬讓，而民不爭；導之以禮樂，而民和睦；示之以好惡，而民知禁。《詩》云：『赫赫師尹，民具爾瞻。』」

Zeng Zi said, "Great indeed is filial respect!"

The Master said, "Filial respect is the constant principle of Heaven, the ultimate standard of Earth, and the code of conduct for the people. This principle of Heaven and Earth serves as a guide for the people. Humans conduct themselves by emulating the brightness of Heaven and making good use of benefits afforded by Earth, so as to bring order to the entire world. Consequently, their teachings, without being severe, are successful; and their government, without being rigorous, secures perfect order.

"The ancient sage-kings noticed that, if they applied this principle (of filial respect) in their teachings, people were transformed; therefore, they first taught people to have loving regard for everyone, and as a result people never neglected their parents; then they taught the virtue of righteousness, and people strove to practice it. They first exemplified themselves in the courtesy of respectful deference, and as a result people did not fight; then by channelling their energy through the rites and music, people were harmonized; and by showing them what to like and dislike, they became aware of the prohibitions. As it is said in the *Book of Poetry:*

> *You are indeed awe-inspiring, Grand-Master Yin,*
> *All people look up to you."*

Notes:

❶ 赫赫：顯盛的樣子。

❷ 師尹：周太師尹氏。

❸ 三才：天、地、人。《易經·說卦》：立天之道曰陰與陽，立地之道曰柔與剛，立人之道曰仁與義，兼三才而兩之，故易六畫而成。

孝治章第八

Chapter 8: Bringing Order into a Kingdom through Filial Respect

子曰：「昔者明王之孝治天下也，不敢遺小國之臣，而況於公、侯、伯、子、男乎？故得萬國之歡心，以事其先王。治國者，不敢侮於鰥寡，而況於士民乎？故得百姓之歡心，以事其先君。治家者，不敢失於臣妾，而況於妻子乎？故得人之歡心，以事其親。夫然，故生則親安之，祭則鬼享之，是以天下和平，災害不生，禍亂不作，故明王之以孝治天下也，如此。《詩》云：『有覺德行，四國順之。』」

The Master said, "In the past when a wise and virtuous ruler reigned over the kingdom with filial respect, he dared not

27

neglect receiving low-ranking envoys from small states, let alone dukes, marquises, earls, counts and barons. In this way, he won the joyous hearts of all the feudal lords; happily they came to pay their respects to the rulers of the past.

"One who governs the kingdom dares not slight or insult widowers or widows, let alone the general citizens or scholars. Therefore, one wins the joyful hearts of the citizens; happily they come to pay their respects to these rulers.

"One who manages the family or clan dares not treat helpers and assistants badly, let alone one's spouses and children. Thus, one wins the joyful hearts of people; happily they attend to their parents.

"In this way, one will be well cared for in life; and after death, one's spirit will enjoy offerings. Thus, all under Heaven will be peaceful, and no calamities or chaos will arise. This is how a wise and virtuous ruler governs the kingdom with filial respect. As it is said in the *Book of Poetry*:

> *With his enlightened virtuous conduct,*
> *He gained the happy following of all."*

Notes:

❶ 封建制爵位五等：公、侯、伯、子、男。

聖治章第九

Chapter 9: The Government of the Sages

曾子曰：「敢問聖人之德，無以加於孝乎？」子曰：「天地之性，人為貴。人之行，莫大於孝。孝莫大於嚴父，嚴父莫大於配天，則周公其人也。昔者，周公郊祀后稷以配天，宗祀文王於明堂，以配上帝。是以四海之內，各以其職來祭。夫聖人之德，又何以加於孝乎？故親生之膝下，以養父母日嚴。聖人因嚴以教敬，因親以教愛。聖人之教，不肅而成；其政不嚴而治；其所因者，本也。父子之道，天性也，君臣之義也。父母生之，續莫大焉。君親臨之，厚莫重焉。故不愛其親而愛他人者，謂之悖德；不敬其親而敬他人者，謂之悖禮。以順則逆，民無則焉。不在於善，而皆在於凶德，雖得之，君子不貴也。君子則不然，言思可道，行思可樂，德義可尊，作事可法，容止可觀，進退可度，以臨其民；是以其民畏而愛之，則而象之；故能成其德教，而行其政令。《詩》云：『淑人君子，其儀不忒。』」

Zeng Zi said, "May I venture to ask, among the virtues of a sage, is there anything greater than filial respect?"

The Master said, "Humans are the noblest living beings between Heaven and Earth, just as filial respect is the loftiest of all virtuous deeds.

"In practicing filial respect, nothing is greater than honoring one's father. In honoring one's father, nothing is greater than according him the same respect one accords to Heaven when performing rites and ceremonies. It began with the Duke of Zhou - he started the practice of performing the rites and ceremonies to both Heaven and his forefather Hou Ji, and performing rites and ceremonies to both the Supreme Lord and his father King Wen in the Hall of Brightness. Those feudal lords, of various ranks, came from 'the four seas' to pay their homage and participate in the rites and ceremonies as well. So, of a sage's virtues, what else could be greater than filial respect?

"Hence, from the days of infancy to the time when one supports one's elderly parents, one's affection for them grows day by day, and develops into serving them with reverence and awe. Proceeding from that awe, the sage teaches reverence for one's parents; from that affection, the sage teaches love for one's parents. Hence, without being severe, the sage's teaching is effective; without being harsh, the sage's governing of a state brings about order. That is because the sage proceeds from the foundation.

"The father-son relationship is a part of the nature of Heaven, resembling that between a ruler and a subject.

"One's parents give birth to one's body, and nothing is more important than carrying on the family's lineage. The father watches over one's development just as a sovereign attends to the affairs of state, and nothing is greater than his kindness. Hence, not to love one's parents but to love others instead is to go against the ethical virtues. Not to revere one's parents but to revere others is to go against propriety. Not to comply with morality but to go against it deprives people of a standard to follow. As a result, they will not be rooted in goodness, but will tend towards evil. They may be able to obtain material benefits or well-paying positions, but a virtuous person will not value these.

"In contrast, a virtuous one will not behave in that way. He will first consider whether his words are praiseworthy, and whether his conduct is a delight to others. His virtues and righteousness are worthy of respect, his exemplary conduct serves as a model for others, his expressions and movements are admirable, his advancing or retreating become the standard for others, and his presence inspires both awe and affection in others who yearn to emulate him. Because of his virtuous example, his teaching becomes successful, thus his governing of the state becomes effective. As it is said in the *Book of Poetry*:

> *The virtuous one, the princely one,*
> *Impeccable is his behavior.*"

紀孝行章第十

Chapter 10: Fivefold Daily Practice of Filial Respect

子曰：「孝子之事親也，居則致其敬，養則致其樂，病則致其憂，喪則致其哀，祭則致其嚴。五者備矣，然後能事親。事親者，居上不驕，為下不亂，在醜不爭。居上而驕則亡，為下而亂則刑，在醜而爭則兵。三者不除，雖日用三牲之養，猶為不孝也。」

The Master said, "When serving his parents at home, a filial son is respectful.

When taking care of them, he is happy.

When his parents are sick, he feels worried.

When they pass away, he is grieved.

When making offerings to them, he is solemn.

With these five aspects perfected, he is considered well qualified to take care of his parents.

"One who serves one's parents well never becomes arrogant when presiding in a high position, never becomes unruly when dwelling in a low position, and never contends when in a disadvantageous situation. Arrogance in high positions leads to one's downfall. Rebelling as a subordinate leads to punishment by the law. Contending under unfavorable circumstances leads to violence. If one does not do away with these three things, then even if one performs rituals to one's ancestors daily with a grand offering of the three precious items, one is still considered unfilial."

五刑章第十一

Chapter 11:The Five Punishments

子曰：「五刑之屬三千，而罪莫大於不孝。要君者無上，非聖人者無法，非孝者無親。此大亂之道也。」

The Master said, "The Five Punishments of the criminal law are meted out for thousands of offenses; but among all those offenses, none is greater than being unfilial.

"One who threatens one's ruler has no regard for one's superiors. One who slanders a sage has no sense of the law. One who slanders the filial conduct of others has no concern for one's own parents or relatives. These acts pave the way to great chaos."

Notes:

❶ 封建制五刑指笞、杖、徒、流、死。

❷ 非孝者無親：譏毀孝行的人可以無父無母。

廣要道章第十二

Chapter 12: An Explanation of "The Essential Way"

子曰：「教民親愛，莫善於孝；教民禮順，莫善於悌；移風易俗，莫善於樂；安上治民，莫善於禮。禮者，敬而已矣。故敬其父則子悅；敬其兄則弟悅；敬其君則臣悅；敬一人而千萬人悅。所敬者寡，而悅者眾，此之謂要道也。」

The Master said, "In teaching people to be friendly and love each other, the first and foremost is to educate them on filial respect.

"In teaching people good etiquette and obedience, instilling fraternal respect is most important. In transforming customs, nothing is more effective than music. In maintaining peace for the ruler and governing the subjects well, nothing is more effective than the teaching of propriety.

"Propriety is essentially about reverence. Therefore, the son is happy when his father is being revered; the younger brother is happy when the elder brother is revered; the subjects are happy when their ruler is revered.

"Revering one person makes millions happy. Few are revered and yet so many are made happy. That is why it is called the ' essential way.'"

廣至德章第十三

Chapter 13: An Explanation of "The Utmost Virtues"

子曰：「君子之教以孝也，非家至而日見之也。教以孝，所以敬天下之為人父者也；教以悌，所以敬天下之為人兄者也；教以臣，所以敬天下之為人君者也。《詩》云：『愷悌君子，民之父母。』非至德，其孰能順民如此，其大者乎？」

The Master said, "A person of character, in his teaching of filial respect, does not necessarily go from house to house, nor does he necessarily see people every day. In teaching filial repesct, the aim is to enable everyone to respect and regard all fathers as one's own father; in teaching fraternal respect, the goal is to enable everyone to respect and treat all brothers as one's own brothers; in teaching the duty of a subject, the purpose is to enable one to respect and treat every ruler as one's ruler.

"As it is said in the *Book of Poetry*:

A peaceful, loving, and gentle person
Is the parent of his people.

"Without the utmost virtues, how could one accord with the masses to such a great extent?"

廣揚名章第十四

Chapter 14: An Explanation of "Leaving a Good Name"

子(zǐ)曰(yuē)：「君(jūn)子(zǐ)之(zhī)事(shì)親(qīn)孝(xiào)，故(gù)忠(zhōng)可(kě)移(yí)於(yú)君(jūn)；事(shì)兄(xiōng)悌(tì)，故(gù)順(shùn)可(kě)移(yí)於(yú)長(zhǎng)；居(jū)家(jiā)理(lǐ)，故(gù)治(zhì)可(kě)移(yí)於(yú)官(guān)。是(shì)以(yǐ)行(xíng)成(chéng)於(yú)內(nèi)，而(ér)名(míng)立(lì)於(yú)後(hòu)世(shì)矣(yǐ)。」

The Master said, "A person of character, who serves his parents with filial respect, can extend this virtue in the form of loyalty towards the ruler; he who serves his brothers with fraternal respect can extend this respect to accord with all his elders; he who manages his household well can extend this management skill to affairs of the state. Hence, when one develops such internal qualities, one's good name will shine throughout future generations.

46

諫諍章第十五

Chapter 15: Remonstrating

曾子曰：「若夫慈愛、恭敬、安親、揚名，則聞命矣。敢問子從父之令，可謂孝乎？」子曰：「是何言與？是何言與？昔者天子有爭臣七人，雖無道，不失其天下；諸侯有爭臣五人，雖無道，不失其國；大夫有爭臣三人，雖無道，不失其家；士有爭友，則身不離於令名；父有爭子，則身不陷於不義。故當不義，則子不可以不爭於父，臣不可以不爭於君。故當不義則爭之，從父之令，又焉得為孝乎？」

48

Zeng Zi said, "I have heard and learned about loving kindness and respect, attending to and caring for the parents, and carrying on the good name of the family. May I ask the Master whether a son who always obeys his father's every command is considered filial?"

The Master replied, "What are you saying? What are you talking about?

"In ancient times, the Son of Heaven who had seven upright ministers or advisors to remonstrate with him would not lose his empire even if he was immoral and negligent. A prince who had five upright advisors to remonstrate with him would not lose his principality even if he did not abide by the principles. A minister who had three upright advisors to remonstrate with him would not lose the nobility of his family, even if he did not abide by the principles. A civil servant who had one upright friend to remonstrate with him would not ruin his reputation. A father who had an upright son exhorting him would not be mired in doing unrighteous acts.

"Therefore, seeing that unrighteous acts are being done or about to be done, the son should never fail to remonstrate with his father, and a minister should never fail to remonstrate with his ruler. Whenever such acts of misconduct are being done or about to be done, remonstrations must be made accordingly.

So, how can you say that being filial is simply obeying a father's every command?"

感應章第十六

Chapter 16: Responses

子曰：「昔者明王事父孝，故事天明；事母孝，故事地察；長幼順，故上下治。天地明察，神明彰矣。故雖天子，必有尊也，言有父也；必有先也，言有兄也；宗廟致敬，不忘親也；修身慎行，恐辱先也；宗廟致敬，鬼神著矣。孝悌之至，通於神明，光於四海，無所不通。《詩》云：『自西自東，自南自北，無思不服。』」

"In the past, the sage-kings were filial towards their fathers and thus served Heaven with understanding. By being filial towards their mothers, they thus served Earth discreetly. The young were compliant towards their elders, and thus there was harmony between superiors and subordinates. Because Heaven was served with understanding and Earth was discreetly gods and spirits manifested and blessed the people. Therefore, even the Son of Heaven had to pay respects to someone, i.e., his father; even he had to defer to someone, i.e., his brothers. One paid ceremonial homage in the ancestral temple to remember one's relatives.

"For fear of disgracing one's ancestors, one cultivated one's character and was cautious in one's conduct. The spirits of one's ancestors came happily to partake of the food that was displayed during the making of sacrifices at the ancestral temple. By perfecting both filial and fraternal conduct, one could evoke responses from ghosts and spirits, and spread one's renown throughout the 'four seas,' reaching all places without any obstruction. The *Book of Poetry* says:

> *From the West to the East,*
> *From the South to the North;*
> *None thought of disobeying."*

事君章第十七

Chapter 17: Serving the Sovereign

子曰：「君子之事上也，進思盡忠，退思補過，將順其美，匡救其惡，故上下能相親也。《詩》云：『心乎愛矣！遐不謂矣！中心藏之，何日忘之。』」

The Master said, "In serving one's sovereign, a virtuous one considers all matters thoroughly. While in office, he thinks about exercising his utmost loyalty; and when retired, contemplates how to rectify his shortcomings and make up for his mistakes. He accords with his sovereign's beneficial undertakings, and seeks to rectify and make amends for his sovereign's shortcomings. In such a way, the sovereign and the subject are both close and cordial towards one another. The *Book of Poetry* says:

> *With a loving heart,*
> *Unhindered by distance,*
> *One keeps him in mind,*
> *Every day, never forgetting.*"

喪親章第十八

Chapter 18: Mourning for Parents

子曰：「孝子之喪親也，哭不偯，禮無容，言不文，服美不安，聞樂不樂，食旨不甘，此哀戚之情也。三日而食，教民無以死傷生。毀不滅性，此聖人之政也。喪不過三年，示民有終也。為之棺、槨、衣、衾而舉之，陳其簠簋而哀慼之；擗踊哭泣，哀以送之；卜其宅兆，而安措之；為之宗廟，以鬼享之；春秋祭祀，以時思之。生事愛敬，死事哀慼，生民之本盡矣，死生之義備矣，孝子之事親終矣。」

The Master said, "When a filial son mourns for his parents, he weeps without wailing, his moves are devoid of the courtesy of details, and his words are devoid of elegance. He feels uncomfortable dressing up in fine clothing and finds no happiness in music, nor does he enjoy good food. Such are the feelings of grief and sorrow. He begins eating again after three days, so as to teach the people not to harm their health because of mourning for the dead, and not to ruin themselves from grieving. Such are the regulations of the sages. His mourning does not exceed three years, so as to show the people that there is a conclusion to all things.

"The body, clothed and shrouded, is lifted into the coffin, and the funeral ceremonial vessels are set out. The grieving relatives beat their chests, stomp their feet and cry sorrowfully in the send-off. A feng-shui diviner is consulted beforehand about the burial site so that the deceased can rest in peace; thereafter, they erect the ancestral temple so as to let the spirits partake of the offerings. They observe each seasonal sacrifice so as to cherish the memories of the dead.

When his parents are alive, the filial son honors them with reverence and affection. After their passing, he mourns for them in sorrow and anguish. Thus, in terms of the service rendered towards the living and the deceased, he has fulfilled his fundamental duty as a citizen. This is the completion of a filial son's duty!"

Notes:

❶ 俙 : 形容哭泣的尾聲悠長。

❷ 簠簋 : 古代祭祀盛稻粱黍稷的器皿。

❸ 擗 : 用手捶拍胸部。

❹ 踴 : 頓足。

創辦人——宣化上人簡傳

A Biographical Sketch of Venerable Master Hsuan Hua

宣化上人，俗姓白。1918年生於中國吉林省雙城縣（現屬黑龍江省），出生前夕，其母夢見阿彌陀佛大放光明。十二歲起，每天早晚向父母叩頭認錯，以報親恩。十九歲母逝，於墓旁結廬守孝三年，人稱「白孝子」；同年禮上常下智老和尚出家，法名安慈，字度輪。

Venerable Master Hsuan Hua was born in 1918 to the Bai family in Shuangcheng County, Jilin Province (now Heilongjiang Province),

China. The night before his birth, his mother dreamed that Amitabha Buddha radiated a brilliant light. At the age of twelve, the Master began bowing every morning and evening to his parents, wishing to repent for his wrongdoings and to repay their kindness. When he was nineteen, his mother passed away. He built a tiny thatched hut next to her grave and lived there for three years as an act of filial respect, thus earning the name "Filial Son Bai". That year he also bowed to the Venerable Master Chang Zhi as his teacher and became a Buddhist monk with the Dharma names An Ci ("Peaceful Kindness") and Du Lun ("Wheel of Salvation").

1948 年仰慕禪宗泰斗上虛下雲老和尚之德行，前往廣州南華寺參禮，雲公觀其為法門龍象，遂任命為南華寺戒律學院監學。次年叩別雲公，前往香港弘法，並建立西樂園寺、慈興禪寺、佛教講堂等道場。1956 年雲公於雲居山，以法脈委付上人為溈仰宗第九代嗣法人，賜法號為宣化。

The Master greatly admired Venerable Elder Master Hsu Yun ("Empty Cloud"), so in 1948 he traveled to Nanhua Monastery in Guangzhou to pay homage to the Elder Master. Elder Master Yun recognized the Master's capacities in the Dharma and appointed him as an instructor at the Nanhua Vinaya Academy. The following year, the Master bid farewell to Elder Master Yun and went to Hong Kong, where he propagated the Dharma and founded Western Bliss Gardens Monastery, Cixing Chan Monastery, and the Buddhist Lecture Hall. In 1956, Elder Master Yun, who was at Yunju Mountain, transmitted the Dharma lineage to the Master, giving him the Dharma name Hsuan

Hua ("Proclaim and Transform") and making him the ninth patriarch of the Weiyang Sect.

1962 年隻身赴美，初期暫住於一地下室中，待緣而化，自號「墓中僧」。1968 年機緣成熟，應華盛頓州立大學三十餘名學生之請，於三藩市佛教講堂，開設暑假楞嚴講修班；九十六天結業後，美籍青年五人懇求剃度出家，隨後到臺灣海會寺受具足戒，這是上人在美國建立僧團之始。

In 1962, the Master traveled to the United States and took up residence in a tiny basement, waiting for the right time to teach. During the time he nicknamed himself "The Monk in the Grave." The right time came in 1968, when thirty-some students from the University of Washington in Seattle went to the Buddhist Lecture Hall in San Francisco to attend a summer study and practice session on the Shurangama Sutra. At the end of the 96-day session, five Americans left the home-life and became monastics. They later traveled to Taiwan and received full ordination, thus becoming the first members of the Sangha that the Venerable Master established in America.

爾後僧團逐漸壯大,上人因而於 1976 年購置佔地 488 英畝的萬佛聖城,做為國際性的大道場。並在城內相繼成立育良小學、培德中學、法界佛教大學、僧伽居士訓練班等教育機構。由於上人德行感人,其後二十餘處分支道場紛紛成立,遍佈美國、加拿大、亞洲及澳洲等地。

The Sangha grew steadily in size, and in 1976 the Venerable Master purchased the 488-acre property of the City of Ten Thousand Buddhas, in order to establish a large-scale, international monastery and community. He founded a series of schools on the campus: Instilling Goodness Elementary School, Developing Virtue Secondary School, Dharma Realm Buddhist University, and the Sangha and Laity Training Programs. As the Venerable Master's virtue inspired more people, twenty-some branch monasteries were established throughout the United States, Canada, Asia, and Australia.

上人畢生的三大志願是弘法、譯經、教育。上人說:「只要我有一口氣在,就要講經說法。」因此數十年如一日,說法不輟。上人又說:「將佛經翻譯成各國語言文字,把佛法播送到每一個人心裏,這才是永遠的。」因此成立譯經院,訓練弟子翻譯經典。

上人對教育的看法是：「教育，就是最根本的國防！」因此積極成立中小學等各種教育機構，培育人才。

The Master's three great, lifelong vows were to propagate the Dharma, translate the sutras, and promote education. He said, "As long as I have a single breath left, I will explain the sutras and speak the Dharma." Thus he explained the Dharma continuously, on a daily basis, for several decades. The Master also said, "To translate the Buddhist sutras into every language and to deliver the Buddhadharma into every person's heart will be a lasting achievement." To this end, he founded the International Translation Institute and trained his disciples to translate sutras. The Master's view of education was that "Education is the best national defense!" He established various types of educational programs to nurture people's talents.

「我從虛空來，回到虛空去。」1995 年，大慈悲普度，流血汗、不休息的上人圓寂了。其實上人的一生，就是一部最感人的真經，只要循著上人的足跡，步其後塵，每個人都可以繼續上人未竟的志業。

"I came from empty space, and I'll return to empty space." In 1995, the Venerable Master passed into stillness after a lifetime of compassionate teaching and diligent, tireless effort. His entire life could be considered the most authentic and inspiring sutra. Anyone who follows in the Master's footsteps can take part in helping to realize the Master's as-of-yet unfulfilled vows.

法界佛教總會簡介

Brief Introduction of the Dharma Realm Buddhist Association

法界佛教總會（以下簡稱法總），係宣化上人所創辦的國際性宗教及教育組織，積極地致力於佛法的研習、修行、教化和實踐。法總凝聚所有四眾弟子智慧與慈悲之力量，以弘揚佛法、翻譯經典、提倡道德教育、利樂有情為己任，俾使個人、家庭、社會、國家，乃至世界，皆能蒙受佛法的薰習，而漸趨至真、至善、至美的境地。

Dharma Realm Buddhist Association (DRBA) is an international religious and educational organization established by the Venerable Master Hsuan Hua. It focuses its efforts on studying, practicing, and teaching the Dharma. Relying on the wisdom and compassion of all members of its Fourfold Assembly, DRBA's missions are propagating the Dharma, translating the Sutras, promoting ethics-based education and benefiting all sentient beings. It is DRBA's wish that every person, family, society, country, and even the whole world can be permeated by the Dharma's edification, and gradually reach the state of ultimate truth, wholesomeness, and beauty.

每位參與法總的四眾弟子，均矢志奉行上人所倡導的六大宗旨：不爭、不貪、不求、不自私、不自利、不打妄語。僧眾則恪遵佛制：日中一食、衣不離體，並持戒念佛，習教參禪，和合共住地獻身佛教。

Every member of DRBA's Fourfold Assembly firmly resolves to practice the Six Great Principles advocated by the Venerable Master: no fighting, no greed, no seeking, no selfishness, no pursuing personal advantage, and no lying. In addition, the Sangha members respect and follow the rules set down by the Buddha, such as eating one meal a day (at midday), always wearing the precept sash, upholding the precepts, reciting the Buddha's name, studying the Dharma, meditating, and devoting their lives to Buddhism while living in harmony with each other.

法總自 1959 年成立以來，相繼成立了二十餘座道場，遍佈美、

亞、澳洲，以距舊金山北部 110 英里的萬佛聖城為樞紐。各分支
道場均遵守上人所立下的嚴謹家風：

Since its founding in 1959, DRBA has successively established over
twenty branch monasteries throughout the U.S., Canada, Asia and
Australia. DRBA's headquarter is located at the City of Ten Thousand
Buddhas, 110 miles north of San Francisco. Every branch monastery
observes the following rigorous standards established by the Venerable
Master:

> 凍死不攀緣，餓死不化緣，窮死不求緣；
> 隨緣不變，不變隨緣，
> 抱定我們三大宗旨。
> 捨命為佛事，造命為本事，正命為僧事；
> 即事明理，明理即事，
> 推行祖師一脈心傳。

> *Freezing to death, we do not scheme;*
> *Starving to death, we do not beg;*
> *Dying of poverty, we ask for nothing.*
> *We accord with conditions, but do not change;*
> *We do not change, yet accord with conditions.*
> *We adhere firmly to our Three Great Principles.*

> *We renounce our lives to do the Buddha's work;*
> *We mold our destinies as our basic duties;*
> *We rectify our lives to fulfill the Sangha's role.*
> *Encountering specific matters, we understand the principles;*

Understanding the principles, we apply them to specific matters.
We carry on the single pulse of the Patriarchs' mind-transmission.

法總的教育機構，有國際譯經學院、法界宗教研究院、僧伽居士訓練班、法界佛教大學、培德中學、育良小學等，除了積極地培養弘法、翻譯及教育之傑出人才外，並推展各宗教間之交流與對話，以促進宗教間的團結與合作，共同致力於世界和平之重責大任。

The educational organizations of DRBA include the International Translation Institute, Institute for World Religion, Sangha and Laity Training Programs, Dharma Realm Buddhist University, Developing Virtue Secondary School, and Instilling Goodness Elementary School. In addition to training outstanding individuals with expertise in propagation of the Dharma, translation and education, DRBA is dedicated to developing and facilitating interfaith dialogue in order to promote harmony and cooperation among the world's religions and work together toward world peace.

法總下的道場及機構，門戶開放，沒有人我、國籍、宗教的分別，凡是各國各教人士，願致力於仁義道德、追求真理、明心見性者，皆歡迎前來修持，共同研習！

All of DRBA's monasteries and institutions have an open-door policy. No distinctions are made based on one's nationality or religion. Anyone who is devoted to developing kindness and virtue, pursuing the truth, and discovering their true nature is welcome to cultivate and explore these issues with us!

育良小學、培德中學簡介
Instilling Goodness Elementary and Developing Virtue Secondary Schools

育良小學、培德中學創辦人宣化上人，中國東北吉林省人。幼年家貧失學，至十五歲始入私塾讀書，兩年半學貫四書、五經、古文及十餘本醫書。因此自十八歲（1936年）開始，在自家創辦義務學校，免費教導鄰近貧苦兒童讀書。此後上人終其一生，見世風日下，道德淪亡，即大聲疾呼、汲汲致力於教育之改革工作。

Venerable Master Hsuan Hua, the founder of Instilling Goodness Elementary and Developing Virtue Secondary Schools, was born in northeastern China. As a young child, he did not have an opportunity to attend school due to his family's financial hardships. It was not until the age of fifteen that he enrolled in a private school. Within two and a half years, he had mastered the Four Books and Five Classics, classical Chinese literature, and a dozen Chinese medical texts. At the age of eighteen (1936), he started a school in his own home and offered free education to the disadvantaged children in his village. Observing the decline in morals, the Venerable Master devoted the rest of his life to speaking out about the need for educational reform and to realizing that goal.

1976 年育良小學在舊金山國際譯經學院成立，以「孝」為宗旨，教育幼童做人的根本道理；1978 年學校遷入清淨寬廣的萬佛聖城。繼而於 1981 年成立培德中學，以「忠孝」為宗旨，進一步教育學生忠於國家。學校除了加州政府規定的正式課程外，並以中國古八德：孝、悌、忠、信、禮、義、廉、恥，教導學生，使他們將來能成為卓越的公民，進而影響整個世界的風氣。

Instilling Goodness Elementary School was founded in 1976 at the International Institute for the Translation of Buddhist Texts in San Francisco, taking filial piety as its core virtue and focusing on teaching children basic moral principles. The school moved to the peaceful and spacious grounds of the City of Ten Thousand Buddhas in 1978. Developing Virtue Secondary School, founded in 1981, had the core virtues of filial piety and service and focused on guiding students to contribute to their nation. In addition to the subjects required by the California state government, the schools emphasize the eight virtues of filial piety, kindness, citizenship, trustworthiness, respect, fairness, integrity, and humility, in the hope that students will become outstanding citizens who will exert a positive influence on the rest of society.

瑜伽市的市民知道有育良、培德之後，逐漸地把子女送來就讀，學生人數因而增多。為了讓學生專心課業，1982 年開始採男女分校制。同時期城中設有難民救濟中心，來自這些佛教家庭的孩子也就讀本校，使學校更增加了國際性的特色。難民中心於 1986 年結束。

As the residents of Ukiah came to know about and send their children to Instilling Goodness and Developing Virtue Schools, the student population grew in size. To allow students to better concentrate on their studies, the schools were divided by gender in 1982. Meanwhile, the City of Ten Thousand Buddhas established the Buddhist Refugee Rescue and Resettlement program (for refugees from the Vietnam war), and children from various Buddhist countries enrolled in the schools, making them more international and diverse in character. The refugee program concluded in 1986.

上人提倡義務教學，因此於 1992 年召募義務老師，他們不受薪，奉獻時間精力，成為本校特色之一。除了正規的學術課程外，佛學課、打坐課、道德課，都是本校最具特色的課程。學校以中文為第二語言，學生被要求能背誦中文或英文之〈弟子規〉。課外尚有國樂、舞龍、舞獅、書法、太極拳、民族舞蹈等極具中國傳統文化之活動。

The Venerable Master advocated volunteer teaching and in 1992 began recruiting volunteer teachers who gave their time and energy to teaching students without taking a salary. Volunteer teachers are one of the features of the schools. Another feature is that in addition to the regular academic courses, the curriculum included courses in Buddhist studies, meditation, and ethics. Students take Chinese as their second language and are required to memorize the Standards for Students [a Confucian text on basic morals] in either English or Chinese. Extracurricular activities include Chinese traditional cultural activities such as Chinese orchestra, dragon dance, lion dance, calligraphy, Taiji [shadowboxing], and folk dance.

此外，學校尚有太鼓、校刊、畢業紀念冊、學生會、模擬聯合國、籃球、足球、瑜珈、鋼琴、小提琴、戲劇、宗教研究、宗教對話、數學競賽、中文學術競賽、郊遊等多元性課外活動，每個學生都參與數項不同之活動。

A variety of extracurricular activities are offered such as Taiko drumming, school newspaper, yearbook, the Associated Student Council, Model United Nations, basketball, soccer, yoga, piano, violin, drama, religious studies, interfaith dialogue, mathematics competitions, Chinese culture competitions, community service, and field trips.

自 1992 年起，上人以「老吾老以及人之老，幼吾幼以及人之幼」的悲懷，指示學校每年在春季舉辦懷少節，邀請鄰近學校學生約四百人一起同樂；在秋季則舉辦敬老節，邀請社區內的老人到萬佛聖城內，由學生表演各項節目，並提供美味可口的素食來招待嘉賓。這兩項活動已受到瑜伽市民眾的肯定與迴響。暑假期間則

72

舉辦青少年夏令營，每年以不同的主題和課程，讓青少年能在佛教道場體驗不同的生活方式，深受歡迎。

Starting in 1992, the Venerable Master promoted the compassionate idea of "respecting your own as well as others' elders and caring for your own as well as others' children," and instructed that the schools celebrate Cherishing Youth Day each spring, inviting hundreds of local school children to participate, and commemorate Honoring Elders Day each fall, inviting local senior citizens to the City of Ten Thousand Buddhas. At these celebrations, students perform for the guests and the kitchen serves them a delicious vegetarian meal. Ukiah residents look forward to these two celebrations every year. Every summer the schools organize a summer camp with a different theme each year, inviting youth to experience a different kind of lifestyle in the monastery, which they find very rewarding.

目前男女校約有一百五十位學生，來自美、亞、歐洲；教職員則有四十二位，大部分是出家和在家的義務老師。學生與老師的比例約為2：1，每班學生約在十人左右，學生因而能得到充分的輔導與關懷。遠道或國際學生，學校備有宿舍，統一作息，培養他們獨立自主的能力。學生並在課餘參與社區服務，如清潔打掃、洗碗盤、協助法會、有機菜園工作等。

Currently about 160 students are enrolled in the schools. They come from North America, Asia, and Europe. There are 42 teachers, the majority of whom are monastics or volunteers. The student-teacher ratio is 2:1. Average class size is ten students, which allows students to receive ample guidance and attention. For international students and students who live too far too commute, the schools offers boarding facilities, where students live communally and learn to be more independent and self-sufficient. Outside of classes, students participate in community service, performing such jobs as cleaning, washing dishes, assisting in Buddhist events, and working at the organic farm.

培德中學期許每位畢業生都能夠：
1. 具有良好的品德，和諧的處世態度，以及領導溝通的能力；
2. 透過打坐及其他靈性的教導與學習，啟發內在本具的智慧；
3. 在學術方面發展各人的潛能和人文、科學、藝術方面的才華；
4. 具有全球性的宏觀胸襟，去欣賞和尊重不同的文化和宗教。

Developing Virtue Secondary School hopes and expects that every graduate can:

1. Manifest the core virtues, interact harmoniously with others, and has developed the skills of leadership and communication.

2. Gain a deep appreciation of their own inherent spiritual wisdom through meditation and other spiritual practices and teachings.

3. Explore and develop their individual academic potential and talents in the humanities, sciences or arts.

4. Express a multinational, global awareness and understanding; and shows an appreciation and respect for a variety of cultures and religions.

培德中學學生在這些薰陶和訓練之後，畢業生已有多人進入加州大學各分校、史丹福大學、哥倫比亞大學、普林斯頓大學、麻省理工學院等名校就讀。有些學生於完成學業後，即回到母校加入義務教師的神聖行列。未來當會有更多的校友，回來擔任教職，使學校朝向薪火相傳的嶄新階段。

After undergoing a transformative influence at the school, many Developing Virtue graduates have been accepted to the various University of California campuses, Stanford University, Columbia University, Princeton University, the Massachusetts Institute of Technology, and outstanding universities. Some alumni, after graduating from college, have returned to their alma mater to join the ranks of volunteer teachers. In the future, even more alumni are expected to come back to take on the responsibility of passing on the school's mission and traditions.

孝經譯者簡介及感言一二
Translators and Feelings

(Compiled in May, 2007)

1、蔡善利

我是 Sunny Chye, 來自新加坡，十六歲。我覺得翻譯《孝經》很有意義，能教導人們如何提高自己的品格。對我語言發展過程中，關係最重要的就是我的母親。從小她就教導我如何從中文翻譯到英文，所以我對翻譯格外有興趣。

最喜歡的名言： " We live our lives with eyes wide shut."

(我們矇著眼珠子過日子)

Sunny Chye: My name is Sunny Chye and I am a 16-year-old from Singapore. I find that translating the *Xiao Jing* very meaningful, because it teaches us how to improve our own characters. The most important person in the development of my language skills is my mother. She taught me how to translate from Chinese to English since young. I am especially interested in translation.

Favorite quote: "We live our lives with eyes wide shut."

2、區景淵

我是 Alex Aw, 今年十七，來自馬來西亞。我翻了《孝經》的第十、十一、十二章。透過翻譯，我漸漸地瞭解了《孝經》；此外，也學到一些翻譯的經驗。我覺得人不唯要讀《孝經》，更重要的是要擁有這些美德。

最喜歡的警句：「一寸光陰一寸金，寸金難買寸光陰。」

「近朱者赤，近墨者黑。」

Alex Aw: I am Alex Aw, 17, and from Malaysia. I translated the tenth, eleventh, and twelfth chapters of the *Xiao Jing*. Through translating this text, I slowly began to understand its meaning. Besides that, I also gained some experience as a translator. I feel that one should not only read the *Xiao Jing*, but to uphold the virtues expressed in it as well. Favorite quote: "An inch of time is an inch of life; an inch of gold can't buy an inch of time."

"One takes on the color of one's company."

3、郭俊佑

我是 Jim Kuo, 譯者之一，生於臺灣臺北，十七歲，負責翻譯《孝經》的第四、五、六章。翻譯《孝經》雖然很有意義，但也是讓我一個頭兩個大。因為近巖師本來只是要十二年級的學長們翻譯，但因為他們太忙，就改成一人翻三章；放完春假，我都居然還沒辦法交差；幸好還可以問 Michael (謝阜庭)，親智也說要幫我。在《孝經》裏，我印象最深的一句話是：「身體髮膚，受之父母，不敢毀傷，孝之始也；立身行道，揚名後世，以顯父母，孝之終也。」我覺得這句話是最好的。至於翻譯，難的地方就有很多；唉！多虧親智幫助，很感激他；現在翻完了，感覺好輕鬆！

我最喜歡的名言：都在《三國演義》中

最喜歡的人物：關公

最喜歡的書：《三國演義》

Jim Kuo: My name is Jim Kuo, a seventeen year old (in 2007) from Taipei, Taiwan. As one of the translators, I was responsible for translating Chapter 4, Chapter 5, and Chapter 6 of the *Xiao Jing*.

Even though translating the *Xiao Jing* is very meaningful, it gives me a huge headache. Originally we were not meant to translate, but because the seniors were too busy to cope on their own, so each person in the class had to translate three chapters. This was very difficult for me because my English is not that good. Thus I was unable to finish translating by the end of the Spring Break. Luckily, Qin Zhi and Michael agreed to help me. Of all the translations, my favorite section was "every part of our bodies, even the hair and skin, is derived from our parents; therefore, we should protect them and keep them from injury; this act is the beginning of practicing filial respect. We establish ourselves by practicing the Way so that we can leave a good name for future generations···this is the fulfillment of filial respect." I think this quote is very profound. Even though translation was very troublesome, I am glad it is over - after having a lot of help from Qin Zhi.

My favorite quotes: (They are all in the *Romance of the Three Kingdoms*.)

My favorite book: *Romance of the Three Kingdoms*

My favorite character: Lord Guan

4、趙子能

我是 Chris Zhao, 17 歲，培德中學 11 年級學生，來自中國大陸。我翻譯《孝經》的第七、八，及第九章。《孝經》翻譯雖然很難，可是很有意義。從來沒有翻過《孝經》，剛開始的的時候感覺有點困難，但後來就比較好。從《孝經》中我學到很多東西；因此我鼓勵大家也翻譯一下《孝經》，從中必能受益良多。

最喜歡的書：《三國演義》

最喜歡的人物：趙雲(趙子龍)

Chris Zhao: I am Chris Zhao, 17 years old, a junior at Developing Virtue Boys School, and an immigrant from Mainland China. I translated the seventh, eight, and ninth chapters of the *Xiao Jing*. Although translating was quite difficult, it was also very interesting. Having never translated this text before, I had some trouble when I first started; however, it got easier as I progressed. I learned a lot from translating the *Xiao Jing*, and I encourage everyone to try it as well; there's much to learn from it!

Favorite book: *Romance of the Three Kingdoms*

Favorite character: Zhao Yun (a.k.a.: Zhao Zilong from the same book)

5、劉親智

我是Qin-zhi Lau，十七歲，「培德中學」十二年級畢業學生。來自於馬來西亞，四歲移民來美。小時候也曾有機會讀到《孝經》，現在又有機會幫忙翻譯這本古籍，很是快樂！希望大家都可以欣賞一下我們那麼多學生辛勞的結晶！（寫於二零零七年五月一日）

最喜歡的書：《三國演義》

最喜歡的名言："The world's a play, and we're all desperately unrehearsed."

（世事如戲，只是倉皇中的你我都沒準備好。）

Qinzhi Lau: I am Qinzhi Lau, 17, 12th grade in Developing Virtue Boys' School (2007). Originally from Malaysia, I moved to America at age four. When I was younger, I once read the *Xiao Jing*. I'm really glad that I had the chance to help translate this great classic. I hope everyone will be able to enjoy the result of the hard work of all these students! (Written on 5/1/2007)

Favorite book: *Romance of the Three Kingdoms*

Favorite quote: "The world's a play, and we're all desperately unrehearsed."

6、謝阜庭

我是謝阜庭，今年十八歲，現在就讀「培德中學」；出生於臺灣，八歲來美國「萬佛聖城」讀書。喜好打球、唱歌、彈琴，也喜歡學習中文。

最喜歡的名言：「坐而言不如起而行。」

Michael Hsieh: I am Michael Hsieh, an 18 year-old student at DVBS; born in Taiwan, I came to America and the CTTB at age eight. I enjoy reading, playing basketball, singing, playing piano, and learning Chinese.

Favorite quote: "Better to rise and act than to sit and speak."

法界佛教總會・萬佛聖城

Dharma Realm Buddhist Association & The City of Ten Thousand Buddhas
4951 Bodhi Way, Ukiah, CA 95482 USA
Tel: (707) 462-0939 Fax: (707)462-0949 http://www.drba.org , www.drbachinese.org

國際譯經學院 **The International Translation Institute**
1777 Murchison Drive, Burlingame, CA 94010-4504 USA
Tel: (650) 692-5912 Fax: (650)692-5056

法界宗教研究院 (柏克萊寺)
Institute for World Religions (Berkeley Buddhist Monastery)
2304 McKinley Avenue, Berkeley, CA 94703 USA
Tel: (510) 848-3440 Fax: (510)548-4551

金山聖寺 **Gold Mountain Monastery**
800 Sacramento Street, San Francisco, CA 94108 USA   Tel: (415) 421-6117 Fax: (510)788-6001

金聖寺 **Gold Sage Monastery**
11455 Clayton Road, San Jose, CA 95127 USA   Tel: (408) 923-7243 Fax: (408)923-1064

法界聖城 **City of the Dharma Realm**
1029 West Capitol Avenue, West Sacramento, CA 95691 USA
Tel: (916) 374-8268 Fax: (916)374-8234

金輪聖寺 **Gold Wheel Monastery**
235 North Avenue 58, Los Angeles, CA 90042 USA Tel: (323) 258-6668 Fax: (323)258-3619

長堤聖寺 **Long Beach Monastery**
3361 East Ocean Boulevard, Long Beach, CA 90803 USA   Tel/Fax: (562) 438-8902

福祿壽聖寺 **Blessings,Prosperity, and Longevity Monastery**
4140 Long Beach Boulevard, Long Beach, CA 90807 USA   Tel/Fax: (562) 595-4966

華嚴精舍 **Avatamsaka Vihara**
9601 Seven Locks Road, Bethesda, MD 20817-9997 USA   Tel/Fax: (301) 469-8300

金峰聖寺 **Gold Summit Monastery**
233 First Avenue, West, Seattle, WA 98119 USA   Tel: (206) 284-6690

金佛聖寺 **Gold Buddha Monastery**
248 E. 11th Avenue, Vancouver, B.C. V5T 2C3 Canada Tel: (604) 709-0248 Fax: (604)684-3754

華嚴聖寺 **Avatamsaka Monastery**
1009 Fourth Avenue S., Calgary, AB T2P 0K8 Canada Tel: (403) 234-0644   Fax: (403) 263-0637

金岸法界 **Gold Coast Dharma Realm**
106 Bonogin Road, Mudgeeraba, Queensland 4213, Australia
Tel: (07) 5522-8788 Fax (07) 5522-7822

法界佛教印經會 Dharma Realm Buddhist Books Distribution Society
臺灣省臺北市忠孝東路六段 85 號 11 樓
11th Floor, 85 Chung-hsiao E. Road, Sec. 6, Taipei, Taiwan, R.O.C.
Tel: (02) 2786-3022, 2786-2474   Fax: (02) 2786-2674

法界聖寺 Dharma Realm Sagely Monastery
臺灣省高雄縣六龜鄉興龍村東溪山莊 20 號
20, Tong-hsi Shan-chuang, Hsing-lung Village, Liu-Kuei, Kaohsiung County, Taiwan, R.O.C.
Tel: (07) 689-3713 Fax: (07)689-3870

彌陀聖寺 Amitabha Monastery
臺灣省花蓮縣壽豐鄉池南村四健會 7 號
7, Su-chien-hui, Chih-nan Village, Shou-Feng, Hualien County, Taiwan, R.O.C.
Tel: (03) 865-1956 Fax: (03)865-3426

佛教講堂 Buddhist Lecture Hall
香港跑馬地黃泥涌道 31 號 11 樓
31 Wong Nei Chong Road Top Floor, Happy Valley, Hong Kong, China
Tel: (2)2572-7644 Fax: (2)2572-2850

般若觀音聖寺 (紫雲洞)
Prajna Guan Yin Sagely Monastery (Formerly Tze Yun Tung Temple)
Batu 5 1/2, Jalan Sungai Besi, Salak Selatan, 57100 Kuala Lumpur, West Malaysia
Tel: (03)7982-6560 Fax: (03)7980-1272

法界觀音聖寺 (登彼岸)
Dharma Realm Guanyin Sagely Monastery (Formerly Deng Bi An Temple)
161, Jalan Ampang, 50450 Kuala Lumpur, Malaysia
Tel: (03) 2164-8055 Fax: (03) 2163-7118

蓮華精舍   Lotus Vihara
136, Jalan Sekolah, 45600 Batang Berjuntai, Selangor, Malaysia Tel: (03) 3271-9439

法緣聖寺 Fa Yuan Sagely Monastery
1, Jalan, Utama, Taman Serdang Raya, 43300 Seri Kembangan,Selangor, Malaysia
Tel: (03) 8948-5688

馬來西亞法界佛教總會檳城分會
Malaysia Dharma Realm Buddhist Association Penang Branch
32-32C, Jalan Tan Sri Teh Ewe Lim, 11600 Jelutong, Penang, Malaysia
Tel: (04)281-7728 Fax: (04)281-7798

觀音聖寺 Kun Yam Sagely Monastery
馬來西亞森美蘭州芙蓉沉香路門牌 166A 郵區 70200
No. 166A Jalan Temiang, 70200 Seremban, Negeri Sembilan, Malaysia.
Tel: 06-7615032

The Classic of Filial Respect

孝經

國家圖書館出版品預行編目資料

孝經＝The classic of filial respect.——
臺北市：法總中文部,2009.04
　面；　公分
中英對照
ISBN 978-986-7328-44-1（平裝）
1.孝經　2.注釋

193.12　　　　　　　　　98003111

西曆二○○九年四月十一日
佛曆三○三六年三月十六日・宣化上人誕辰日恭印

發行人　法界佛教總會・佛經翻譯委員會・法界佛教大學
地　　址　Dharma Realm Buddhist Association &
　　　　　The City of Ten Thousand Buddhas（萬佛聖城）
　　　　　4951 Bodhi Way, Ukiah, CA 95482 U.S.A.
　　　　　Tel:（707）462-0939　Fax:（707）462-0949

　　　　　The International Translation Institute
　　　　　1777 Murchison Drive
　　　　　Burlingame, CA 94010-4504 U.S.A.
　　　　　Tel: (650) 692-5912　Fax: (650) 692-5056

出　　版　法界佛教總會中文出版部
地　　址　台灣省台北市忠孝東路六段 85 號 11 樓
　　　　　Tel:（02）2786-3022　Fax:（02）2786-2674

倡　　印　法界佛教印經會　　地址／電話:同上
　　　　　法界文教基金會　　高雄縣六龜鄉興龍村東溪山莊 20 號
　　　　　www.drbachinese.org ／ www.drba.org